CLASSIFICATION

Anita Ganeri

Heinemann
LIBRARY

www.heinemann.co.uk
Visit our website to find out more information about Heinemann Library books.

To order:

 Phone 44 (0) 1865 888066

 Send a fax to 44 (0) 1865 314091

Visit the Heinemann Bookshop at www.heinemann.co.uk to browse our catalogue and order online.

First published in Great Britain by Heinemann Library, Halley Court, Jordan Hill, Oxford OX2 8EJ a division of Reed Educational and Professional Publishing Ltd. Heinemann is a registered trademark of Reed Educational & Professional Publishing Ltd.

OXFORD MELBOURNE AUCKLAND
JOHANNESBURG BLANTYRE GABORONE
IBADAN PORTSMOUTH (NH) USA CHICAGO

Designed by Celia Floyd
Originated by Dot Gradations
Printed in Hong Kong/China

ISBN 0 431 10920 6 (hardback)   ISBN 0 431 10927 3 (paperback)
06 05 04 03 02 01   06 05 04 03 02 01
10 9 8 7 6 5 4 3 2   10 9 8 7 6 5 4 3 2 1

British Library Cataloguing in Publication Data

Ganeri, Anita
  Classification. – (Living things)
  1. Biology – Juvenile literature 2. Natural history – Classification – Juvenile literature
  I. Title
  578'.012

Acknowledgements

The Publishers would like to thank the following for permission to reproduce photographs:

Bruce Coleman: Hans Reinhard pg.24; *Mary Evans Picture Library*: pg.4; NHPA: Martin Harvey p.5, pg.29, Laurie Campbell pg.6, pg.9, MI Walker pg.6, Andy Rouse pg.7, ANT pg.8, pg.23, Stephen Dalton pg.8, pg.16, pg.20, pg. 28, Alberto Nardi pg.10, EA Janes pg.11, Daniel Zupanc pg.12, Anthony Bannister pg.13, pg.15, pg.28, NA Callow pg.14, GI Bernard pg.16, John Shaw pg.17, Norbert Wu pg.18, Daniel Heuclin pg.19, pg.22, pg.25, LUTRA pg.21, Christophe Ratier pg.25, Nigel J Dennis pg.27; *Photodisc*: pg.7, pg.26;

Cover photograph reproduced with permission of Bruce Coleman/Alan Stillwell.

Every effort has been made to contact copyright holders of any material reproduced in this book. Any omissions will be rectified in subsequent printings if notice is given to the Publisher.

Any words appearing in the text in bold, **like this**, are explained in the glossary.

Contents

What is classification   4

Five kingdoms   6

Plants without flowers   8

Flowering plants   10

Invertebrates   12

Arthropods   14

Arachnids   16

Fish   18

Amphibians   20

Reptiles   22

Birds   24

Mammals   26

More mammals   28

Glossary   30

Index   32

Introduction

The six books in this series explore the world of living things. *Classification* looks at how scientists use a special system for identifying and naming living things. It explains how they sort living things into groups, based on the features they have in common.

What is classification?

There are millions of living things on Earth. Scientists call them '**organisms**'. But they need a way of telling all the living things apart. To do this, they sort them into groups. This is called classification. It is like the system you use to look for a book in a library. Each book has a number or code to make it easier to find.

Two names

A Swedish scientist, called Carl von Linné (1707–1778), invented the system scientists use today. He gave each living thing a two-part name. The two parts work like your first name and surname. They tell you what the living thing is and which group it belongs to. The ancient language of **Latin** is used for the names. This is so that everyone can understand them, no matter which language they normally speak. For example, the Latin name for a tiger is *Panthera tigris*.

Carl von Linné.

Common names

Many living things have a common name, as well as a scientific (Latin) name. But sometimes two different animals have the same common name. For example, badgers are different in the USA and Europe. You use their scientific names to tell them apart.

How does classification work?

Scientists sort living things into groups. All the living things in a group look alike or have features in common. Start at the bottom and the groups go up in steps like a ladder. You can see them below.

- Kingdoms – the biggest groups.
- Phyla (**singular**: phylum) – similar classes are grouped into phyla.
- Classes – similar orders are grouped into classes.
- Orders – similar families are grouped into orders.
- Families – similar genera are grouped into families.
- Genera (singular: genus) – similar species are grouped into genera.
- **Species** – the smallest groups.

Tiger classification

This table shows the classification for a tiger.

Kingdom:	Animals
Phylum:	**Chordates**
Sub-phylum:	**Vertebrates**
Class:	Mammals
Order:	**Carnivores**
Family:	Cats
Genus:	*Panthera*
Species:	*tigris*

A tiger.

Did you know?

Scientists have classified about two million species of living things. But there may be ten times more still waiting to be discovered.

Five kingdoms

The largest group of living things is called a kingdom. Scientists usually sort living things into five different kingdoms.

Monerans

Monerans are living things such as **bacteria**. Their bodies are made up of only one **cell**. The cells are tiny and much simpler than the cells of other living things. They do not have a **nucleus**. There are over 3000 **species** of monerans.

Protists

Protists are tiny living things. For example, an amoeba is a protist. Their bodies are made of a single cell. The cells have a nucleus. There are more than 28,000 species of protists. They live in water and damp places.

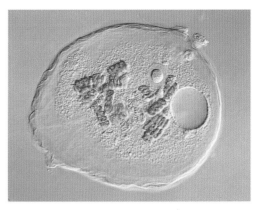

An amoeba.

Fungi

Moulds, mushrooms, toadstools and mildew are all types of fungi. A fungus is made up of tiny threads. It feeds on other **organisms** which can be alive or dead. The threads spread over the fungus's food and suck up the goodness. There are about 75,000 species of fungi.

A fly agaric fungus.

Plants

There are more than 400,000 species of plants. Plant cells have tough walls made of **cellulose**. Plant leaves contain a green substance called **chlorophyll**. It soaks up sunlight. Plants use sunlight to turn **carbon dioxide** from the air and water from the ground into food.

Animals

Animal cells do not have tough walls. Animals cannot make their own food. Most move around to find food. There are about 1,500,000 species of animals.

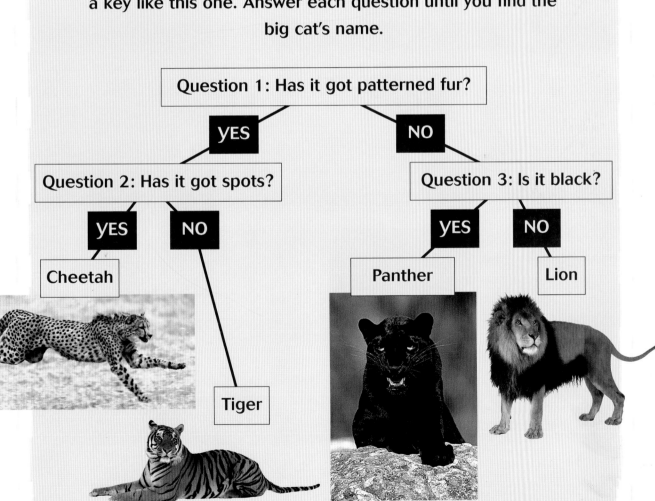

Big cat key

If you do not know what an animal is, you can find out by using a key like this one. Answer each question until you find the big cat's name.

Question 1: Has it got patterned fur?

YES — Question 2: Has it got spots?
- YES → Cheetah
- NO → Tiger

NO — Question 3: Is it black?
- YES → Panther
- NO → Lion

Plants without flowers

The plant kingdom can be split into two groups. They are plants with flowers and plants without flowers. Most plants without flowers grow from tiny specks called **spores**. A plant makes thousands of spores. It releases them into the air and the wind blows them away. If the spores land in a good place to grow, they sprout into new plants.

Algae

Algae are very simple plants. They do not have flowers, roots, stems or leaves. Algae may be red, green or brown. They usually grow in water. Some algae are tiny and made of just one **cell**. But giant seaweeds are types of algae too. These seaweeds grow along the coast.

Giant kelp seaweed.

Mosses and liverworts

Mosses and liverworts are small plants that live in damp places. They make their spores in a tiny **capsule**. The capsule is held up on a thin stalk. When the capsule opens, the spores blow out. The wind carries them away.

A spore capsule of a star moss.

Ferns

Ferns are plants with **frond**-like leaves. They also grow from spores. Some ferns have rusty spots under their leaves. These are where the spores are made.

A type of conifer called a monkey-puzzle tree.

Conifers

Conifers are trees such as pines, redwoods and larches. Conifers do not have flowers. But they do not grow from spores. Conifers grow new plants from seeds. The seeds grow in woody cones. There are about 550 **species** of conifers.

Did you know?

A lichen is a cross between an alga and a fungus. The alga makes food for the fungus. In return, the fungus protects the alga and provides it with water.

Simple Plants		Ferns and Horsetails		Conifers	
Kingdom:	Plants	Kingdom:	Plants	Kingdom:	Plants
Phylum:	Bryophytes – plants with roots, stems and leaves but no **vascular tissue**	Phyla:	Ferns; horsetails; clubmosses – plants with vascular tissue	Phyla:	Conifers; cycads; ginkgoes – trees that grow from seeds
Classes:	Liverworts; mosses; hornworts				

Flowering plants

Many plants have flowers. A plant's flowers are where its seeds are made. These seeds grow into new plants. Inside a flower are the plant's male and female parts. The male parts are called **pollen**. The female parts are called **ovules**. The two parts must join together to make a seed. This is called **pollination**. Some flowers pollinate themselves. Other plants use the wind, or insects or birds to carry pollen from one flower to another.

One leaf or two?

There are two types of flowering plants. They are called monocotyledons (monocots) and dicotyledons (dicots). A cotyledon is a tiny leaf inside a seed. It contains a store of food for the new plant to use. Monocots have only one of these leaves in their seeds. They include plants such as irises and daffodils. They have narrow leaves and three parts to their

A field of poppies. Poppies are dicotyledons.

flowers. Dicots have two leaves in their seeds. They include plants such as poppies and roses. They have broad leaves and four or five parts to their flowers.

Trees

Trees are plants with tall, woody trunks. Conifers (see page 9) are trees that make seeds but do not have flowers. Broadleaved trees have flowers and seeds. Some broadleaved trees change colour and lose their leaves once a year.

A beech tree changing colour in autumn. A beech tree is a broadleaved tree.

Flowering plants	
Kingdom:	Plants
Phylum:	Angiosperms – plants with flowers and fruits
Classes:	Monocots – plants with one leaf in seed (eg: daffodils)
	Dicots – plants with two leaves in seed (eg: roses)
Number of **species**:	more than 250,000

Invertebrates

Invertebrates are animals that do not have a backbone or a skeleton inside their bodies. There are about 950,000 **species** of invertebrates. They are sorted into many different groups. The groups include insects (see page 14), worms, starfish, jellyfish and molluscs.

An edible snail.

Molluscs

Snails, slugs, clams, mussels, octopuses and squid are all types of molluscs. Molluscs are the second biggest group of invertebrates, after insects. All molluscs have soft bodies that are often protected by hard shells. Some molluscs have one shell. Others have two parts to their shells. Most molluscs live in water.

Jellyfish and sea anemones

Jellyfish, sea anemones and corals are close relations. They all have soft, circular bodies. Their mouths are ringed by stinging tentacles that they use for catching **prey**. The box jellyfish from Australia has a deadly sting. It can kill a person in four minutes.

Worms

Some worms have long, tube-shaped bodies, divided into **segments**. Earthworms usually live underground. The burrows they dig help keep the soil healthy. The burrows let air and water flow through the holes in the soil.

Starfish and sea urchins

Starfish and sea urchins have spiny skins and five parts to their bodies. Many starfish have five arms. If a starfish loses an arm, it can grow a new one. Tiny tentacles grow under each arm. The starfish uses the tentacles to move about and catch its prey.

A starfish and a sea urchin.

Invertebrates	
Kingdom:	Animals
Major phyla:	1 Jellyfish and sea anemones
	2 Sponges
	3 Flatworms
	4 Roundworms
	5 Molluscs
	6 Segmented worms
	7 Arthropods

Molluscs	
Kingdom:	Animals
Phylum:	Molluscs
Classes:	1 Chitons
	2 Snails and slugs
	3 Clams and mussels
	4 Squid and octopuses
Number of species:	about 75,000

Arthropods

Insects, arachnids (see pages 16–17), crustaceans, centipedes and millipedes are all arthropods. Arthropods have bodies divided into **segments** and legs that bend at joints. Their soft bodies are covered with hard cases or shells. Most arthropods have **antennae**.

Identifying insects

Insects live all over the world. All insects have three parts to their bodies – the head, **thorax** and **abdomen**. They have six pairs of legs. Most insects can fly. Some have two pairs of wings. Others have only one pair. Insects have large, round eyes. The eyes are made up of hundreds of tiny lenses. Insects have one pair of antennae which they use for smelling, touching and tasting things.

Insects	
Kingdom:	Animals
Phylum:	Arthropods
Class:	Insects
Number of species:	about 1 million

A honeybee is an insect.

Crustaceans

Crabs, lobsters, barnacles, water fleas, shrimps and woodlice are all crustaceans. Crustaceans have bodies divided into segments. Each segment has a pair of legs for walking and swimming. Crustaceans have two pairs of antennae. Most have hard shells. There are about 44,000 **species** of crustaceans.

Centipedes and millipedes

Centipedes and millipedes have very long bodies. Their bodies are divided into many segments. Centipedes and millipedes look quite alike. But centipedes have only one pair of legs on each segment. Millipedes have two pairs. Millipedes are plant-eaters. Centipedes are fierce hunters. There are about 11,000 species of centipedes and millipedes.

A millipede.

Did you know?

There are more different kinds of insects than all other kinds of animal put together. Scientists know of at least one million species. Another 8–10,000 new species are being discovered each year.

Arachnids

Spiders, scorpions, ticks and mites are all arachnids. Arachnids are **invertebrates**. Arachnids are also arthropods. They have two parts to their bodies – the **cephalothorax** (the head and chest joined together) and a large **abdomen**. Arachnids have four pairs of legs and do not have wings or **antennae**.

Spider spinners

Spiders are famous for making silk. The silk is made inside the spider's body and comes out through tiny nozzles called spinnerets. Some spiders use silk to make webs to catch their **prey**. Other spiders chase their prey on the ground, then bite and kill it with their poison fangs. There are about 35,000 **species** of spiders.

A spider eating a tree frog.

A desert scorpion.

Scorpions

Scorpions have four pairs of legs. They also have a pair of strong pincer-like claws for grabbing prey. Many scorpions have poisonous stings in their tails. There are about 800 species of scorpions.

Arachnids get their name from an Ancient Greek myth. Princess Arachne boasted that she could weave better than the goddess Athene. They had a contest and Arachne won. Athene was so angry that she turned Arachne into a spider.

Ticks and mites

Ticks and mites live on other animals and plants and feed on their blood, fur, feathers and **sap**. Ticks and mites can spread deadly diseases in humans, animals and food crops. There are about 30,000 species of ticks and mites. Most are tiny, often less than 1 millimetre long.

A wood tick.

Arachnids	
Kingdom:	Animals
Phylum:	Arthropods
Class:	Arachnids
Number of species:	about 75,000

Fish

Fish are **cold-blooded vertebrates**. Vertebrates are animals that have a backbone and a skeleton inside their bodies. They live in fresh and salty water. They have **streamlined** bodies for swimming, and fins instead of limbs. Fish are **cold-blooded**. This means that they rely on the temperature of the water to warm up or cool down. Fish were the first vertebrates on Earth. The first fish lived about 515 million years ago.

Rubbery skeletons

Sharks, rays and skates have skeletons made of rubbery **cartilage** instead of bone. The great white shark is famous for its razor-sharp teeth and because it sometimes eats people. But the biggest shark is the whale shark. This giant can grow up to 18 metres long. It eats tiny sea plants and animals.

A reef shark.

Bony fish

Bony fish have skeletons made of bone. Herrings, salmon, eels and carp are all bony fish. Bony fish live all over the world, from huge oceans to tiny ponds. The longest bony fish is the oarfish. It can grow over 15 metres long. It is silver with a long, red fin growing along its back. More than 95 per cent of all fish are bony fish.

How fish breathe

Fish use **gills** to breathe **oxygen** dissolved in the water. A fish swims along and opens its mouth. It gulps in water. Then it closes its mouth and pushes the water out through its gills. The gills take oxygen from the water.

Did you know?

The seahorse is a strange shape but it is still a fish. It is related to sticklebacks and pipefish. Seahorses are weak, slow swimmers. They have to cling to seaweed with their tails to stop themselves from being washed away.

Seahorses.

Fish	
Kingdom:	Animals
Phylum:	**Chordates**
Classes:	1 Jawless fish
	2 Fish with skeletons of cartilage
	3 Bony fish
Number of species:	about 24,000

Amphibians

Amphibians are **cold-blooded vertebrates**. Their young live in water and breathe through **gills** like fish. Adult amphibians live on land. They breathe through **lungs**. They also breathe through their moist skins. Frogs, toads, newts and salamanders are all types of amphibians.

Frogs and toads

Frogs and toads look very alike. But there are several ways of telling them apart. Frogs have longer legs and smoother skin than toads. Toads have squatter bodies and some have warty skin. Most frogs and toads live near water. They mostly eat insects and spiders. There are about 3800 **species** of frogs and toads. Scientists discover about 20 new species every year.

A common frog.

Newts and salamanders

Newts and salamanders live in damp undergrowth near ponds and streams. They eat slugs, snails and worms. Newts and salamanders have long bodies, short legs and long tails. If a newt or salamander loses its tail, it can soon grow a new one. There are about 360 species of newts and salamanders.

A fire salamander.

Caecilians

Caecilians look like small snakes but they are amphibians. They have long, tube-shaped bodies and do not have legs. They live in water or burrow in soft earth and feed on insects and earthworms. Most are about 50 centimetres long, but some grow to 1.5 metres long. There are about 170 species of caecilians.

Amphibians	
Kingdom:	Animals
Phylum:	**Chordates**
Class:	Amphibians
Number of species:	about 4500

Reptiles

Snakes, lizards, crocodiles, tortoises and turtles are all reptiles. Reptiles are **cold-blooded vertebrates**. They live mostly on land. Their scaly skin protects their bodies and stops them drying out. Most reptiles lay eggs with tough, leathery shells. Some reptiles give birth to live young. There are about 6500 **species** of reptiles.

Snakes and lizards

Snakes and lizards make up the biggest group of reptiles. There are about 6000 species of them. Lizards range in size from tiny geckos to the huge Komodo dragon. It lives in Indonesia. It can grow more than 3 metres long. The longest snake is the reticulated python. It lives in South-east Asia and can grow as long as six bicycles.

A cobra with its eggs.

Crocodiles

Crocodiles and alligators have strong armour plates on their backs. The plates are made from scales and bones. Crocodiles are fierce hunters. They tear their **prey** apart with their sharp, pointed teeth. Crocodiles are excellent swimmers. Their eyes and nostrils are on top of their heads so that they can lie underwater but they can still see and breathe.

Turtles and tortoises

Turtles, tortoises and terrapins have bony shells to protect their bodies. They have beak-like jaws instead of teeth. They live in water and on land, and feed on plants and small animals. The oldest land animal was a tortoise. It lived to be 152 years old.

Reptiles	
Kingdom:	Animals
Phylum:	**Chordates**
Class:	Reptiles
Number of species:	about 6500

Did you know?

The strange-looking tuatara lives in New Zealand. It is the only survivor of a group of reptiles that lived millions of years ago, at the time of the dinosaurs. The tuatara has a spiky crest growing along its tail and back. Its name means 'peaks on the back'.

A tuatara.

Birds

All birds have beaks, wings and feathers. Most birds can fly, though not all. Many birds have hollow bones to make them lighter in the air. All birds lay eggs, often in nests. Birds are **warm-blooded vertebrates**. This means that they can stay warm and active even if the weather is cold. Birds live all over the world, from the baking deserts to the icy poles.

Perching birds

The biggest group of birds is the perching birds. These are birds such as sparrows and crows. Perching birds have four toes on their feet for gripping tightly on to branches.

The painted bunting is a perching bird.

Birds	
Kingdom:	Animals
Phylum:	**Chordates**
Class:	Birds
Number of species:	more than 8500

The first bird lived about 150 million years ago. It has the **Latin** name *Archaeopteryx* which means 'ancient wings'. It was about the size of a pigeon and had feathers and wings. But it also had teeth and a bony tail, like a reptile.

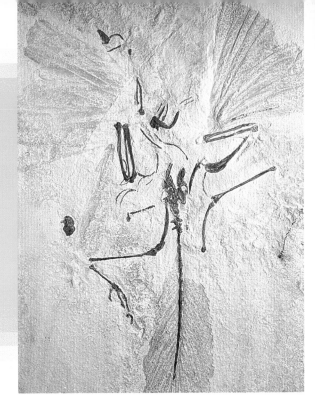

An *Archaeopteryx* fossil.

Runners and swimmers

Some birds have wings but they cannot fly. Ostriches are the largest birds in the world. They are too heavy to fly but they can run at 70 kilometres an hour, faster than a racehorse. Penguins cannot fly. They use their wings like fins to swim underwater. Some penguins can swim three times faster than humans to find fish to eat and escape from hungry seals.

An ostrich running.

25

Mammals

Mammals are **warm-blooded vertebrates**. They breathe air through **lungs**. All mammals have some hair or fur and earflaps on their ears. Mammals look after their babies and feed them on milk. There are more than 4000 **species** of mammals. Elephants, bats, kangaroos and human beings are all mammals.

Mammal pouches

Marsupials are mammals with pouches. Kangaroos, koalas and wombats are all marsupials. Their new-born babies are tiny and weak. They crawl into their mother's pouch where they feed on milk and grow bigger.

Kangaroos have pouches.

Egg-layers

The duck-billed platypus, the long-beaked echidna and the short-beaked echidna are very unusual mammals. They lay eggs. A duck-billed platypus lays her eggs in a riverbank tunnel. When the babies hatch, she feeds them on milk.

Mammals	
Kingdom:	Animals
Phylum:	**Chordates**
Class:	Mammals
Sub-classes:	1 Egg-layers
	2 Non egg-layers
Infra-classes:	1 **Placental**
	2 Non-placental
Number of species:	more than 4000

Mammal groups

Order	Examples	No. of Species
Artiodacytyls	Camels, pigs, cattle	c 180
Carnivores	Cats, bears, dogs	c 250
Cetaceans	Whales, dolphins	72
Chiropterans	Bats	c 800
Dermopterans	Flying lemurs	2
Edentates	Anteaters, sloths	29
Hyracoids	Hyraxes	c 6
Insectivores	Moles, shrews	c 350
Lagomorphs	Rabbits, hares	c 60
Marsupials	Kangaroos, koalas	c 275
Monotremes	Platypus, spiny anteater	3
Perissodactyls	Tapirs, rhinos, horses	15
Pholidotes	Pangolins	7
Pinnipeds	Seals, sea lions, walrus	34
Primates	Lemurs, monkeys, humans	c 200
Proboscids	Elephants	2
Rodents	Mice, porcupines, beavers	c 1750
Sirenians	Dugongs, manatees	4
Tubulidentates	Aardvark	1

Did you know?
The aardvark is an ant-eating mammal. It lives in the **grasslands** of Africa. It burrows for food with its long, spade-like claws and its strong back legs. The aardvark is the only mammal in its order, the Tubulidentates.

An aardvark.

27

More mammals

Most mammal babies grow inside their mothers' bodies. When they are born, they look like miniature versions of their parents. They are called **placental** mammals. This means that while they are growing inside their mothers, they get food and **oxygen** from her body. Whales, bats and human beings are placental mammals.

A bat.

Flying mammals

Bats are the only mammals that can really fly, although some mammals are good gliders. A bat's wings are made from its hands and arms. Its finger bones are very long and have leathery skin stretched between them. The bat's wings are also attached to its back legs and tail.

Did you know?

The African elephant is the largest land mammal in the world. An adult male elephant stands 3 metres tall and weighs more than 5 tonnes. Amazingly, its closest mammal relative is believed to be the rabbit-sized hyrax.

Hyraxes.

Sea mammals

Whales, dolphins, seals, sealions, walruses, sea cows and manatees are all sea mammals. Sea mammals spend their whole lives in or near the sea. The biggest sea mammal is the blue whale. It can weigh 130 tonnes and grow more than 30 metres long. It is the largest mammal that has ever lived.

Human mammals

Human beings are mammals called primates. Primates are sorted into two groups. One group includes bush-babies and lemurs. The other group includes apes (chimpanzees, gorillas, orang-utans, gibbons), monkeys and humans. Human beings are very closely related to apes.

Young chimpanzees.

Human beings	
Kingdom:	Animals
Phylum:	**Chordates**
Class:	Mammals
Order:	Primates
Species:	*Homo sapiens* (humans)

Conclusion

Think how hard it would be to find a book in a library if all the books were jumbled up together. You need some way of sorting them out. This is why classification is so useful. It helps you identify the millions of living things so that you can find the one you want.

Glossary

abdomen   the back part of an insect's or arachnid's body

antennae   feelers on an insect's head. The insect uses them for touching, tasting and smelling.

bacteria   tiny living things that are found almost everywhere. They are made of only one cell.

capsule   a case or container

carbon dioxide   a gas found in the air

carnivore   an animal that eats meat

cartilage   a rubbery material. It makes the skeletons of some fish such as sharks.

cell   tiny building block that makes up the body of all living things

cellulose   tough material in plant cell walls

cephalothorax   the front part of an arachnid's body. It is made of its head and thorax joined together.

chlorophyll   green colouring found in plant cells. It helps the plant to make its own food.

chordates   animals that once had a stiff line of cells in their backs instead of a backbone

cold-blooded   an animal that cannot control the temperature of its body. It relies on the weather to warm it up or cool it down. Many cold-blooded animals cannot live in cold places. They need to be warm to move about and search for food.

frond   a feathery leaf

gill   part of a fish's or young amphibian's body used for breathing in oxygen from the water

grasslands   huge, open spaces covered in grass and bushes

infra-classes   two special sub-classes found only in mammals

invertebrate   an animal that does not have a backbone or skeleton inside its body

Latin   an old language once spoken in Ancient Rome. It is used in science to name living things.

lung   part of an animal's body used for breathing oxygen from the air

nucleus a tiny round speck inside a cell. It controls everything that happens in the cell.

organism a living thing

ovule the female part of a plant or animal

oxygen a gas in the air. Living things need to breathe in oxygen to stay alive.

placental mammals whose babies grow inside their mothers' bodies until they are ready to be born

pollen tiny grains of powder that are the male parts of a plant

pollination the way pollen is carried from a male flower to a female flower or from the male part of a flower to the female part

prey animals that are hunted and killed by other animals for food

sap juices inside a plant that carry food and water

segment a piece or section

singular a single thing. For example, the singular of cats is cat.

species a group of organisms that have similar features and can breed together

spores tiny, dust-like specks made by fungi and other plants without flowers. They grow into new plants.

streamlined having a smooth shape for cutting through the air or water

thorax the middle part of an insect's body

vascular tissue narrow tubes inside a plant. They carry food and water around the plant.

vertebrate an animal with a backbone and skeleton inside its body

warm-blooded an animal that can control its own body temperature. This means it can live in hot and cold places and still stay active and alert.

Index

amphibians   20–1

arachnids   16–17

arthropods   14–15

birds   24–5

classes   5, 9, 11, 13, 14, 17, 19, 21, 23, 24, 26, 29

common names   4

crustaceans   15

families   5

fish   18–19

frogs and toads   20

fungi   6

genera   5

human beings   29

insects   12, 14, 15

invertebrates   12–13, 16, 30

kingdoms   5, 6–7, 9, 11, 13, 14, 17, 19, 21, 24, 26, 29

Linné, Carl von   4

mammals   26–9

molluscs   12, 13

monerans   6

orders   5, 27, 29

organisms   4, 6, 31

phyla   5, 9, 11, 13, 14, 17, 19, 21, 23, 24, 26, 29

plants   7, 8–11

protists   6

reptiles   22–3

scientific (Latin) names   4

scorpions   16

snakes and lizards   22

species   5, 6, 7, 12, 17, 20, 21, 22, 26, 31

spiders   16, 17

ticks and mites   17

trees   9, 11

vertebrates   18, 20, 22, 24, 26, 31